THE
LITTLE GIANT BOOK
OF

Visual Tricks

THE DIAGRAM GROUP

Sterling Publishing Co., Inc.
New York

Library of Congress Cataloging-in-Publication Data Available

Image research by Patricia Robertson

10 9 8 7 6 5 4 3 2 1

Published by Sterling Publishing Co., Inc.
387 Park Avenue South, New York, NY 10016
A Diagram Book first created by Diagram Visual Information
Limited of 195 Kentish Town Road. London NW5 2JU, England
© 2001 by Diagram Information Visual Limited
Distributed in Canada by Sterling Publishing
%o Canadian Manda Group, One Atlantic Avenue, Suite 105
Toronto, Ontario, M6K 9E7, Canada

Sterling ISBN 0-8069-7709-4

Foreword

Seeing is believing? Not anymore. Open this book at any page and blow your mind! Don't study too many of these brain-bending puzzles at once – it could seriously damage your head. See the impossible; see the incredible; witness the wonderful; and give yourself a headache.

In this book you will find a selection of the world's finest eye-tricking, mind-mangling, brain-bashing puzzles, tricks and visual oddities. How can a man be happy and sad at the same time? How can a picture make you seasick? When is a straight line bent? Don't know? Look through these pages and you'll wish you had never asked.

There are hidden objects and lost people to find; mazes to unravel and impossible objects to comprehend. You will have to learn that your eyes are liars if you are going to get through this book without your head melting! Good luck, and remember – when you just can't take any more, all the answers are in the back.

You'll find puzzles like these inside:
Hidden objects
Double meanings
Hidden errors
Optical distortions
Spatial confusions
Distorted pictures

NEW AND ORIGINAL VISUAL TRICKS

Puzzles that start a fight
between your eyes
and your brain

DON'T TRUST YOURSELF

Don't be fooled –
what you see is not
what you think you see

Some puzzles **TORMENT YOUR BRAIN** while others **TORMENT YOUR EYES**

This book will cause your **BRAIN** to **COMPLAIN** about the **LIES** from your **EYES**

1 Around the disk there are thirteen baseball players. Tilt the disk and there are only twelve. Where did the other batsman go?

2 The shop assistant said that all of the
lamps were different. Can you find two
that are the same shape and pattern?

3 Can you read this message?

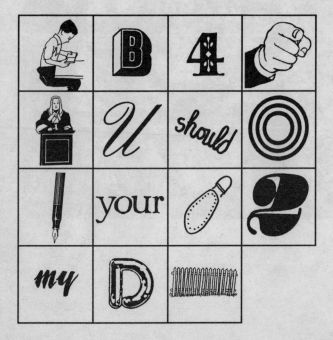

4 Which is closer to the line – the spider or the butterfly?

5 How many legs has this happy hippo got?

6 How many people are at the party?

7 Is she a blonde or a brunette?

8 How could these construction workers have built this building?

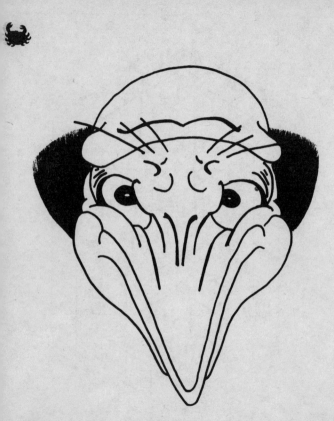

9 Can you find my brother? He is very happy!

10 What's weird about this building?

11 The huntsman is calling the animals from the forest. How many can you find?

A

12 Which circle contains squares –
A or B?

B

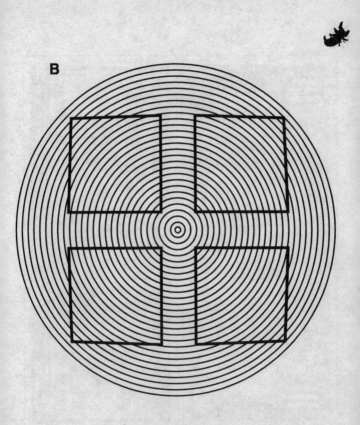

13 Are there any fakes? And if so, can you find the forger's mistakes?

14 Why do you feel seasick when you look at these pages?

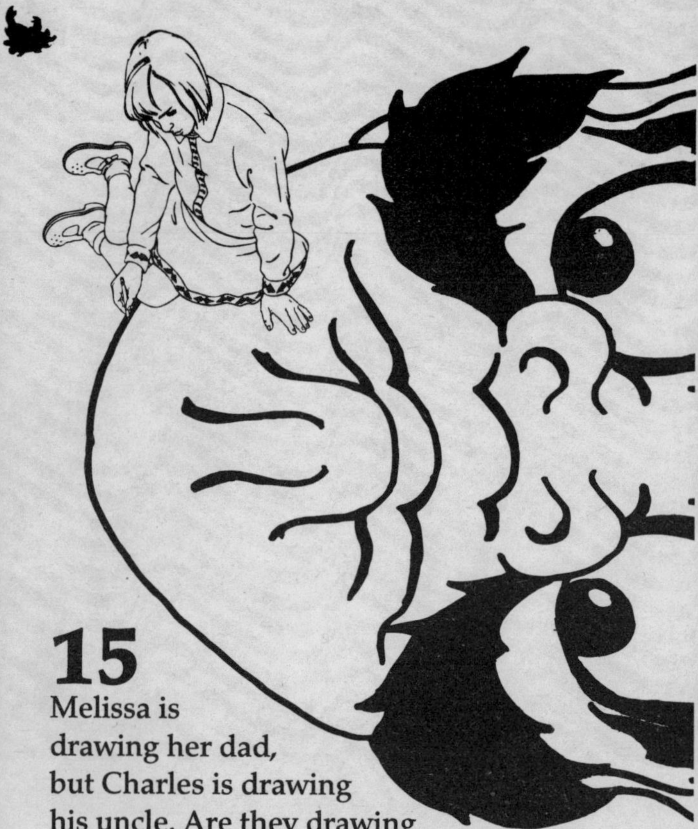

15
Melissa is
drawing her dad,
but Charles is drawing
his uncle. Are they drawing
the same person?

16 Does your brain say it's got gray lines across it side to side and top to bottom?

17 Mr. Egghead is looking for Mr. Rabbit. Can you help find the rabbit?

18 Two lovers meet at a lakeside. Can you find them?

19 What does this say?

20 How many letters can you find in this pattern?

21 Which bomber is bigger?

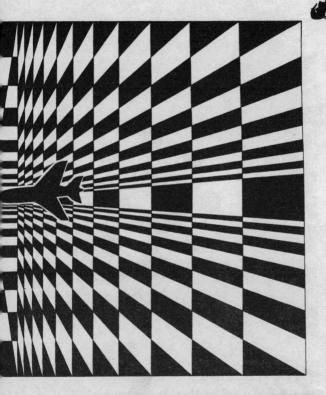

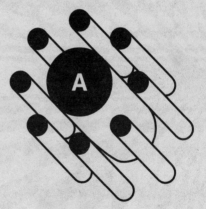

22 Peter had to select either A or B as the larger bucket. Which bucket would you choose?

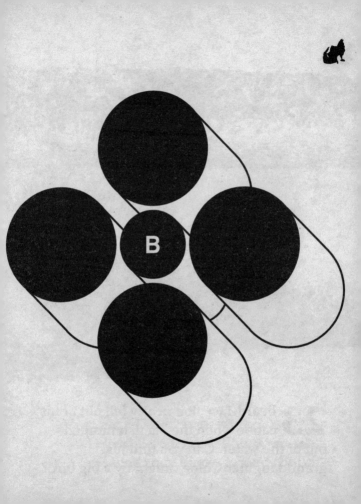

23 Beard-face Bob nearly fell out of his canoe when the big fish jumped out of the water. Can you find his granddaughter Chloe caught by a big bird?

His granddaughter
Chloe screamed when
the big bird got her.

24 There are six differences between the State seals on this page and those on the next. How many can you find?

25 This sign outside the store has a mistake. Can you spot it?

WE'VE
GOT A
A BIG
SALE
NOW

26 How can the space traveler turn into a bandit?

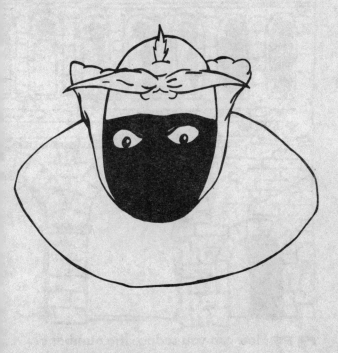

27 How can you reduce the number of lower arches to only four?

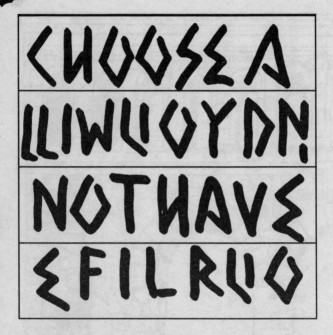

28 The ancient Greeks wrote their words in opposite directions on each line. Can you read this example?

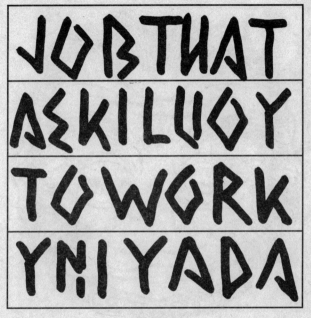

29 How does this leprechaun turn into a sumo wrestler?

30 Are there really gray patches at the corners of the black squares?

31 Potbelly Bill is trying to find his younger brother, Frank. Can you help him?

32 Which spoon is larger?

33 George Washington got lost in the woods while searching for his cat. Can you find them both?

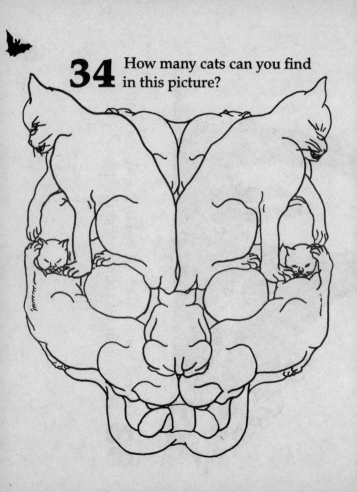

34 How many cats can you find in this picture?

35 A professor in Mexico discovered a hoard of gold rings, each one bearing the image of a monkey. One, he decided immediately, was a forgery. Can you spot the fake?

A

B

C

D

E

F

G

H

I

J

K

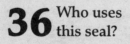

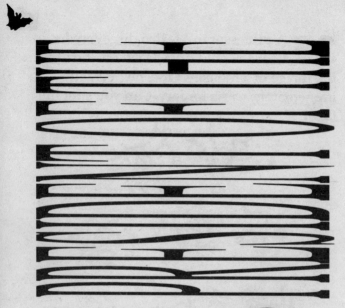

36 Who uses this seal?

UNITED STATES OF AMERICA

37 How can you have five candles filling a seven-candle holder?

38 Is this guy happy or unhappy?

39 Do the lines on the disks slope down to the left or down to the right?

40 Do the sides of the arches join in the middle?

41 How many blocks are used in these shapes?

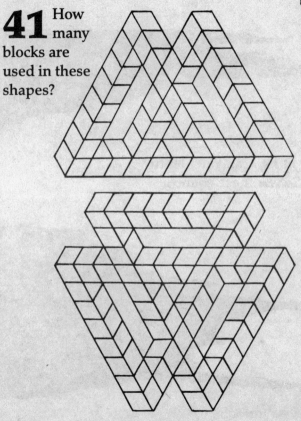

42 Can you identify these countries?

43 Bob insists that his poles are the same distance apart at the top and bottom.

Lauren insists her poles are too.

Who is right?

44 Is the fly on the top side of the log, or the bottom side?

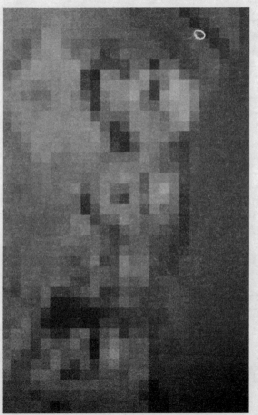

45 Can you tell what this is?

46 Paul's mom is calling him. Can you see where Paul is hiding?

47 Do you know what part of the world these shapes belong to?

48 Is this a spiral? Try following one of the lines round to see.

49 This Arab girl has a very angry father. Can you see him?

50 Which of the twelve dice is a fake?

51 There are sixteen differences between this picture and the one on the next two pages. How many can you see?

51 Look at the last two pages. Can you find the sixteen differences?

52 Peter spent a long time building his shapes out of sand. On the next page are the shapes that Martha made. How are they different?

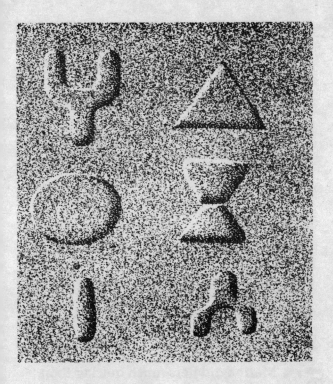

52 Martha did hers much quicker than Peter's on the previous page by pressing them into the sand. What is the difference between Martha's shapes and Peter's?

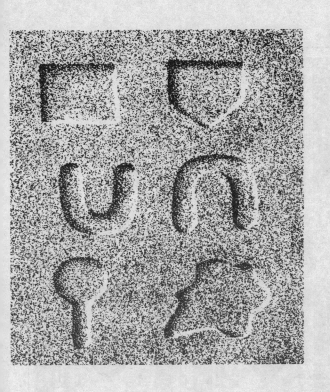

53 Which one is real?

54 Are these hoops circular?

55 Can you see the patterns formed by the lines?

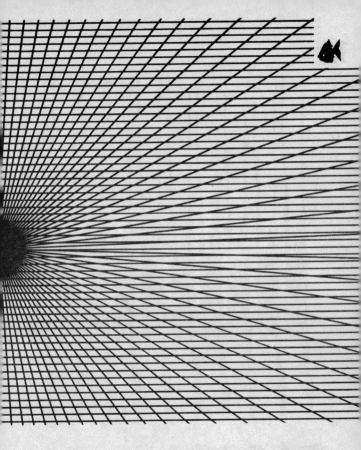

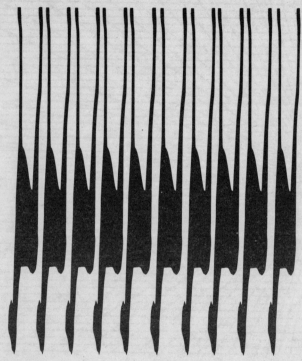

56 What are these?

57 This is a sign on a glass door. What does it say?

58 This design has two straight lines across it. Or does it?

59 There are twelve differences
between these two pictures.
Can you find them all?

60 Is the shape at the center the letter B or the number 13?

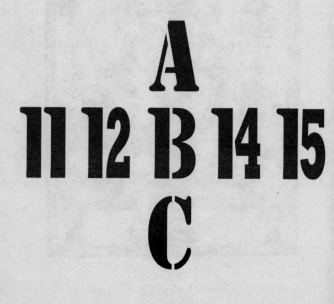

61 This monkey likes hanging around. Can you find his owner?

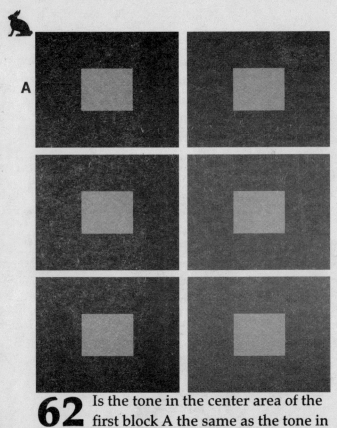

62 Is the tone in the center area of the first block A the same as the tone in the center of the last block B?

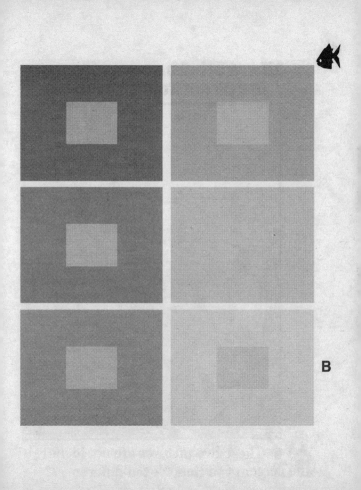

B

63 These two pictures are not identical. Can you find the ten differences?

Wer recht bescheyden wol werden
Der pit got auff erden trum hye

10 15

64 Can you find two sisters in the woods?

65 Which clowns have the longer ropes?

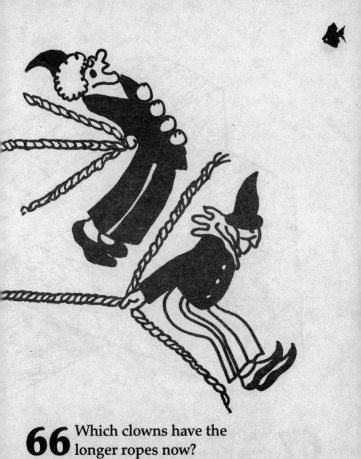

66 Which clowns have the longer ropes now?

67 Where would you drill a hole to fix these three pieces of wood together?

68 Do these two pages look flat?

69 Where is this?

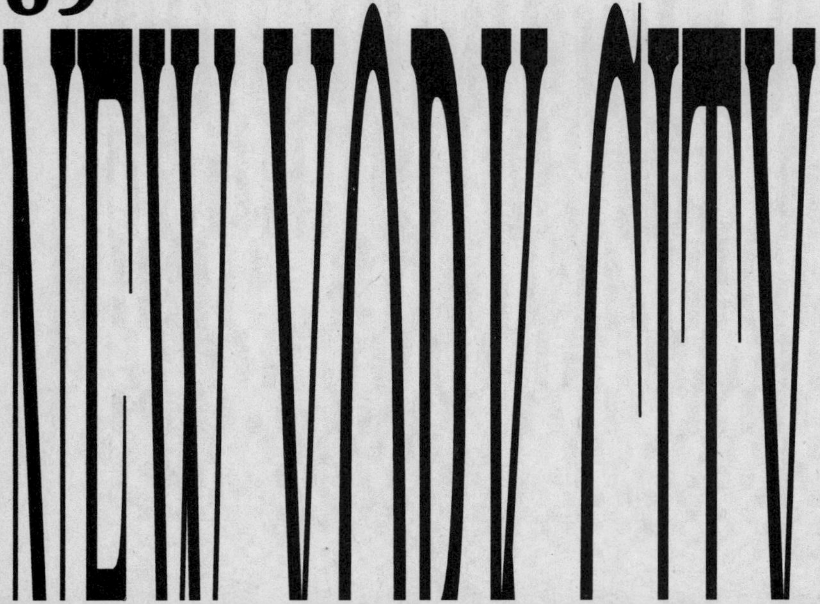

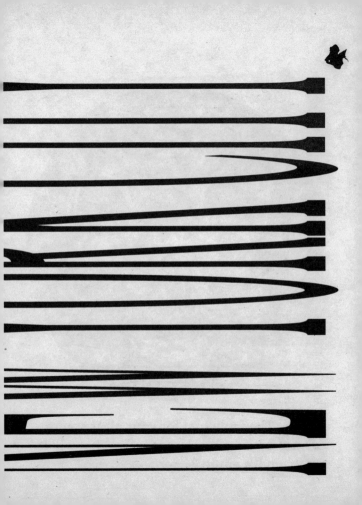

70 The table mat for your glass smiles when your glass is full. What will it do when it's empty?

71 Everyone at the wedding is looking for Grandpa. Can you find him?

72 Is David seeing bottles or glasses?

73 What is this?

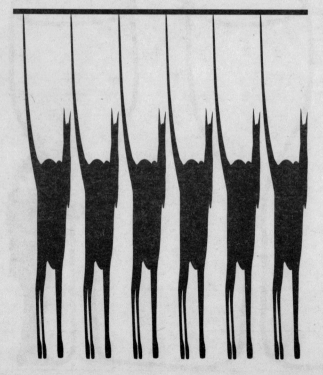

74 Can you read this message?

75 Is the dot in the center of the circle?

76 Which pen is longer – top or bottom?

77 Can you spot the seven differences between these two pictures?

79 Which two figures have inner circles that are the same shade of gray?

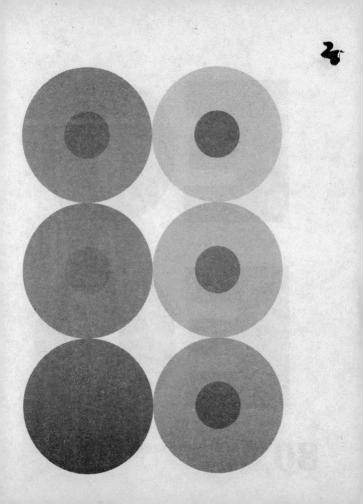

80 Which O is the same height as the E next to it?

81 Is this a place or a person?

82 Are there any fakes?

83 Which of these pencil scribbles is longer?

84 Two cryptic messages:

This is the best way to get a job done. What does it say?

2
T

8
M

This is another way to describe where something originates from! What is the word?

85 Which S and which 8 is the same width at the top as it is at the bottom?

86 Can you spot nineteen differences between these two pictures?

87 Could you make a box like this?

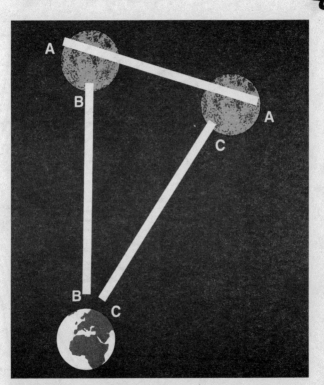

88 Which line is longer than the other two? A–A, B–B, or C–C?

89 Stare at the black hole and the lines bend. Or are they already bent?

90 Beard-face Bob climbed down the ladder. "Come on down," he called.

His granddaughter Chloe was afraid she would fall. What happened?

91 How are these boxes arranged?

93 There are eight differences between these two pictures. Can you see them?

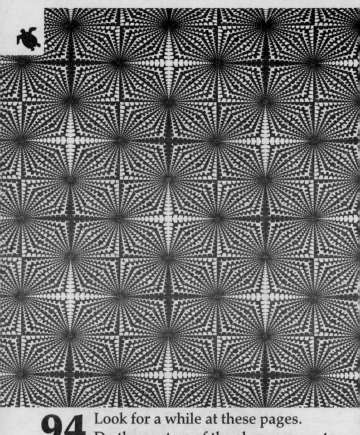

94 Look for a while at these pages.
Do the centers of the shapes seem to
have a gray fuzz around them?

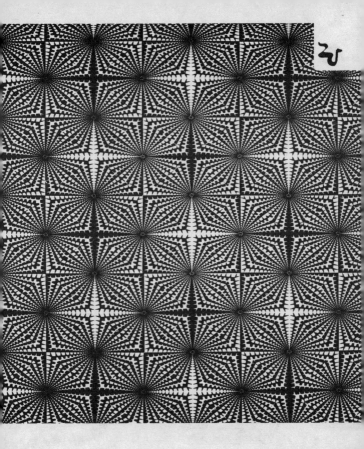

95 Does this picture
appear strange
to you?

96 Which wallpaper pattern has stripes with the same width all the way along?

97 Two friends go sailing and one falls overboard. Can you find him?

98 Can you spot the twenty differences between these two pictures?

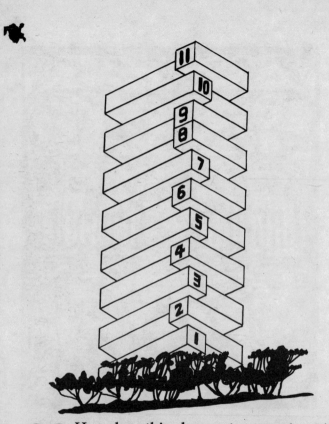

.99 How does this eleven-story apartment block only have eight balconies?

100 Can you help this man to find the burglar hiding in his house?

101 Which U.S. state is this?

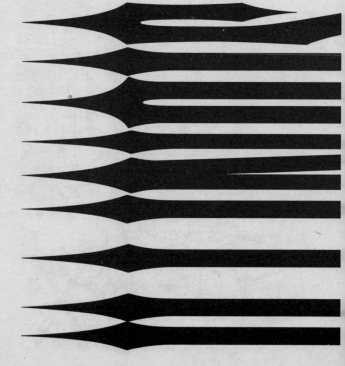

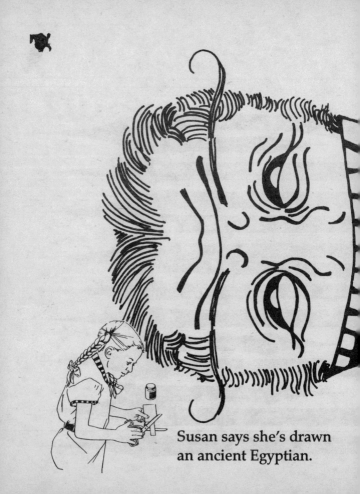

Susan says she's drawn
an ancient Egyptian.

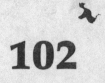

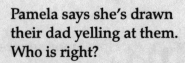

Pamela says she's drawn
their dad yelling at them.
Who is right?

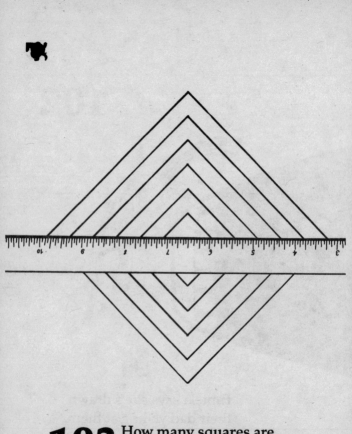

103 How many squares are there under the rulers?

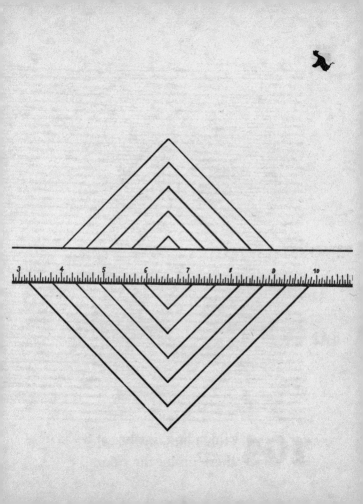

104 Which line finishes at B – is it A1 or A2?

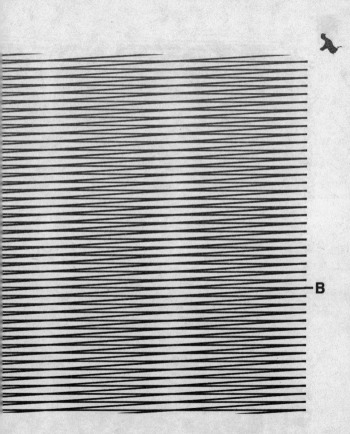

B

105 Can you find the twelve differences between this picture and the one on the next two pages?

Look at the previous two pages. How many of the twelve differences can you find?

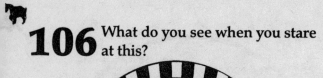

106 What do you see when you stare at this?

107 Which man is larger – A or B?

108 What words do these people spell with their shapes?

109

Sam is trying to count how many dice there are. Can you help?

Joseph is counting the
dice from this side. How
many are there?

110 Why are Tom and Lenny having trouble building their barn?

111 When you turn over the page the circles turn into ovals – or do they?

111 Ovals or circles?
See the previous page.

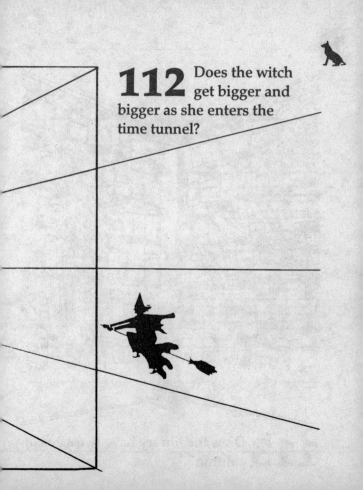

112 Does the witch get bigger and bigger as she enters the time tunnel?

113 Does the library have two sizes of column?

114

These hunters are searching for animals in

the forest. How many can you find?

115

What does the sign on the doors mean?

116 What is unusual about these scissors?

117 The Egyptian king wanted to have the larger pyramid for his family. Which did he choose?

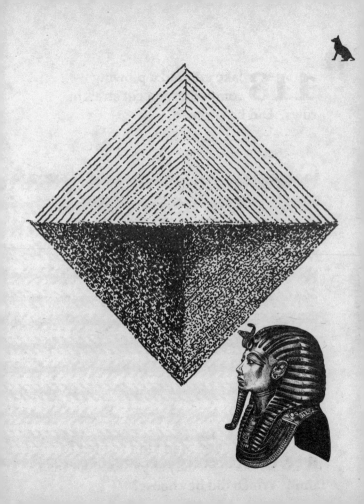

118
Jake entered a plowing competition to cut straight rows. Did he succeed?

119 Can you read this message?

IMITATION IS THE SINCEREST FORM OF FLATTERY

120 Where are the five people admiring these flowers?

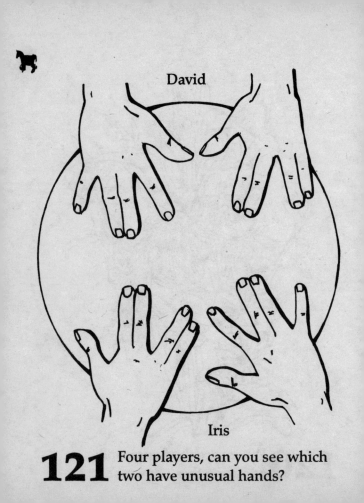

David

Iris

121 Four players, can you see which two have unusual hands?

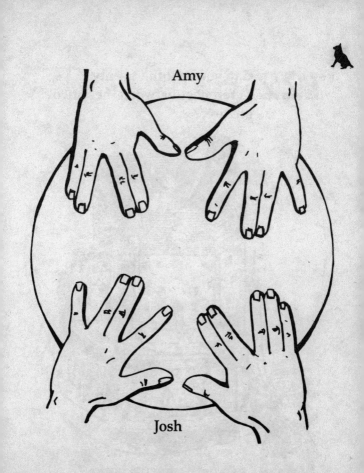

122 Can you spot the twenty differences between these two pictures?

123

When Peter goes fast does the mark on his tire travel in a circle?

124 Melissa wants to add another block. Can she?

125 This horse is afraid of frogs. Can you find the frog in the stable?

126

If these cars both drive at the same speed, where will they meet?

127 Can you read these shapes?

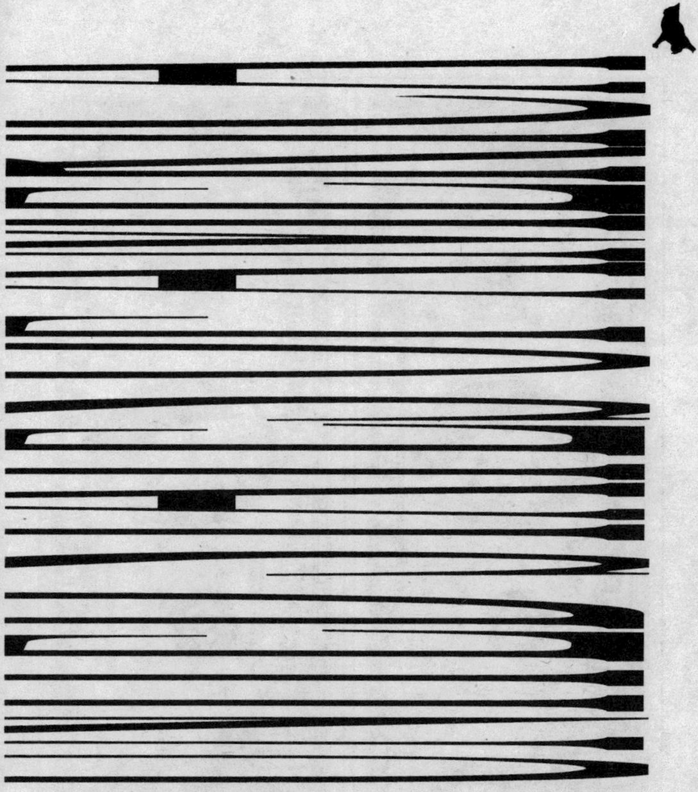

128 Are there any fakes?

129 This young girl will one day be an old lady. Can you see her in this picture?

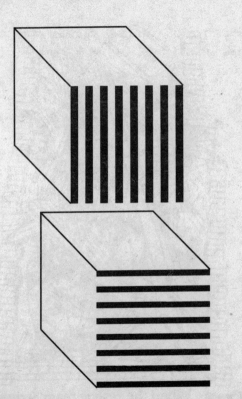

130 Which box is the taller of the two and which one is the wider?

131 When the rescue team arrived they found Mr. Brown and his daughter. Can you find their cat and dog?

132 The masked lady is looking for her bearded cowboy. Can you find him?

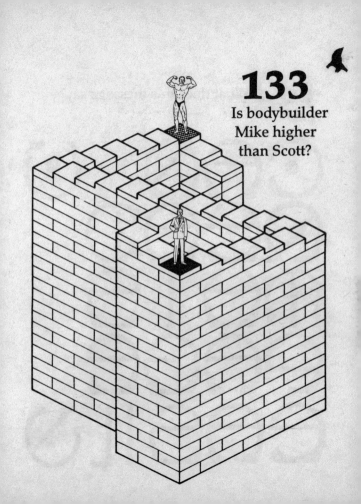

133
Is bodybuilder
Mike higher
than Scott?

134 What does this message say?

135 Is there something wrong with this bed?

136 John's watchstrap had broken so he carried the watch in his pocket. As he entered the station his watch showed 5:21 – but he had missed his 7:50 train. Why?

137 How many children can you count in this fight?

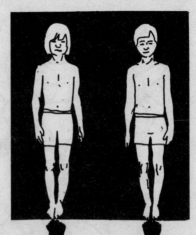

138
Which are
bigger –
the children
or their
shadows?

139 Are these rings circular?

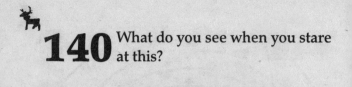

140 What do you see when you stare at this?

141 George can't read this. Can you?

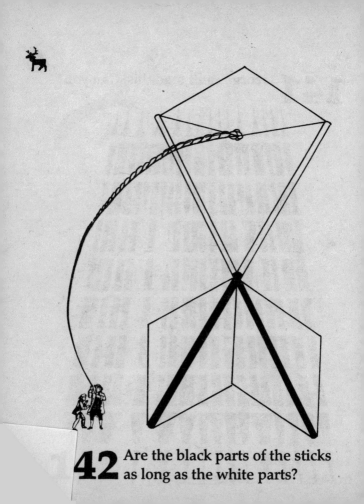

42 Are the black parts of the sticks as long as the white parts?

143 Can you see six people admiring these flowers?

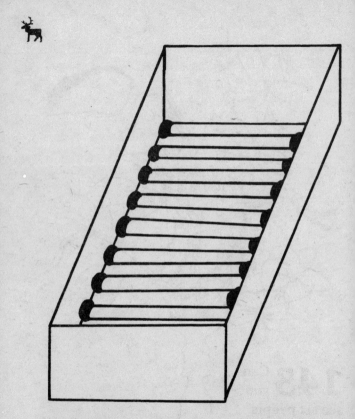

144 How many matches are there in this box?

145

Which stack of coins is as wide as it is tall – A or B?

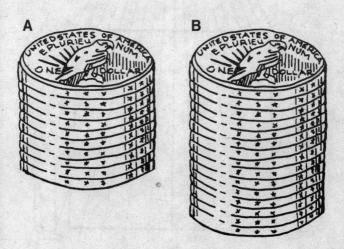

A

B

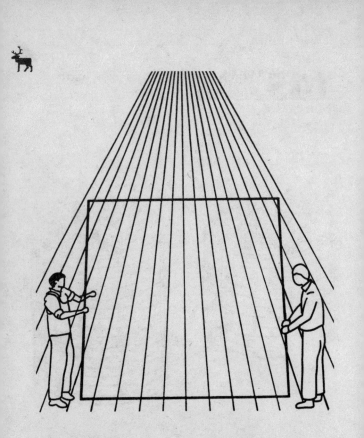

146 Are these men carrying a square piece of glass?

147

Where is the
magician?

1961

148 What is so special about 1961?

149

A square box – will the hat fit in upright or sideways?

150 Can you identify this country?

151

**Who are
these two
people?**

152 Are any of these shapes circles?

153 Is the ant inside the maze unable to get out? Is it able to escape without climbing over a wall?

154 One of these printed circuits has a fault. Can you find it?

155
What do you see if you agree with someone?

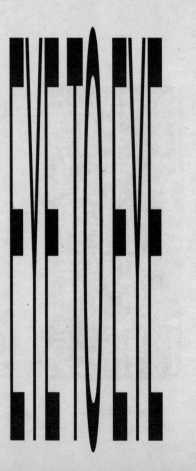

156
Two of
these cards are
forgeries, which
ones?

157 Can you recognize this artist?

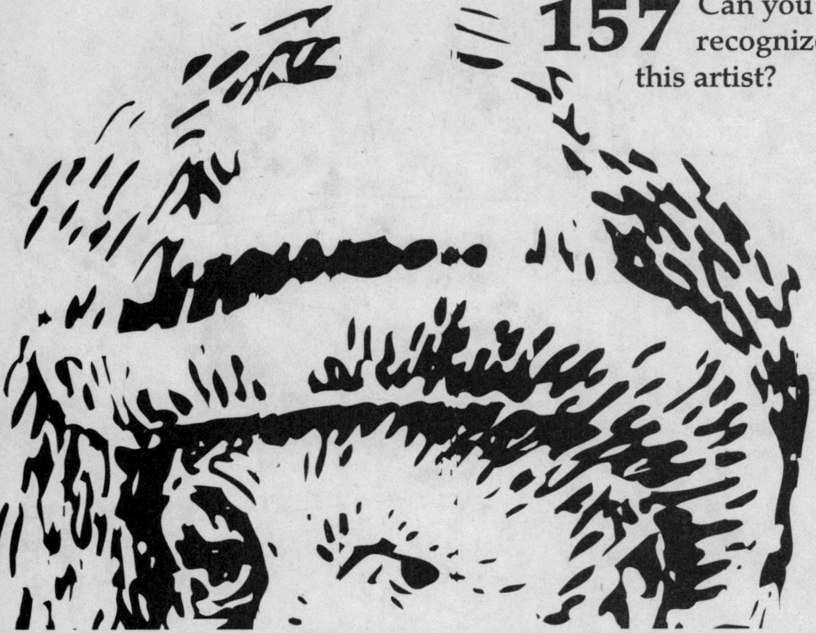

158 Which rectangle has a dot in the center?

159

What does
this sign
say?

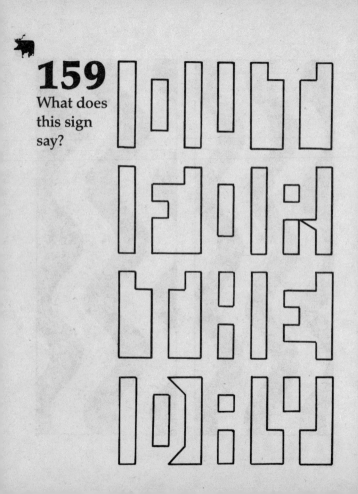

160 Can you follow the spiral down to the center?

161 What do these shapes mean?

162 What does this shape mean?

163 Is this lady alone?

164 Which box contains two straight vertical lines – the left or right?

165 Can you spot the naturalist?

166 Are these circles?

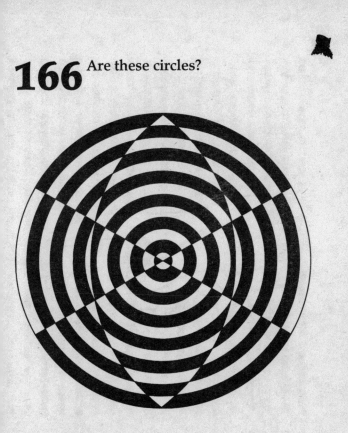

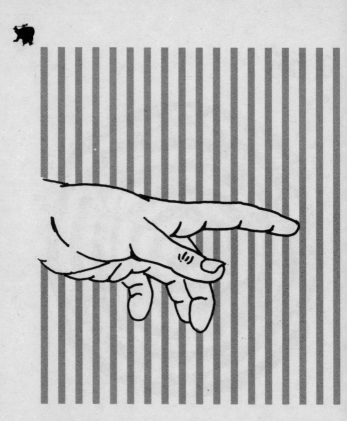

167 Try moving these hands closer to your eyes and see what happens.

168 For his final examination, Abraham produced perfectly accurate drawings of the front and side views of a solid object. What shape was the object?

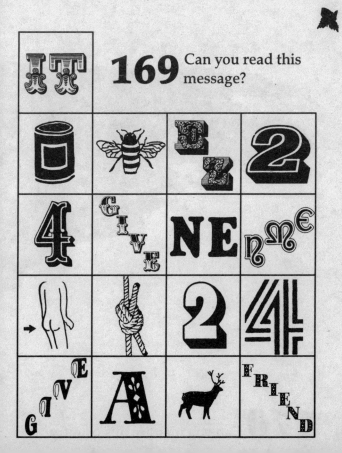

169 Can you read this message?

170 Can you identify this country?

171 Do the holes on these pages spin clockwise or counterclockwise?

172 Can you read these two messages?

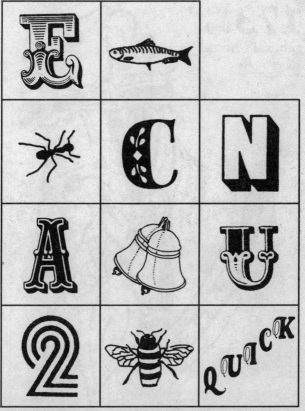

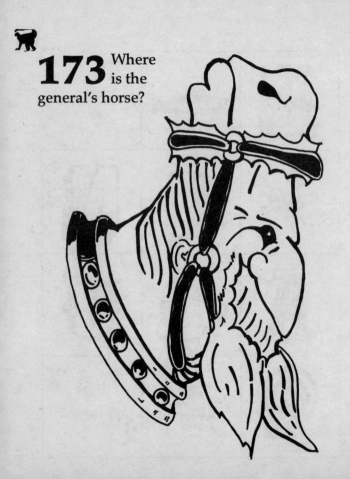

173 Where is the general's horse?

174 What can you see in this pattern?

175

Lee says that
Ogg, the forest
demon, is angry.

Kay thinks
that Ogg
is happy.
Who is right?

176 What can you see when you look at this pattern?

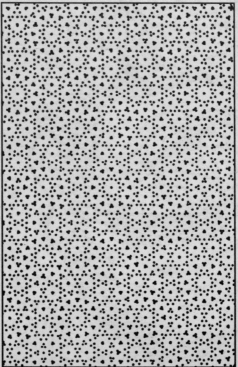

177 Could you interlock these frames like this?

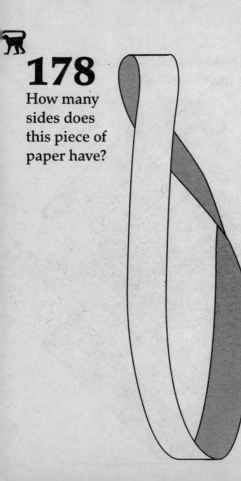

178
How many sides does this piece of paper have?

179 Which book is bigger than the other two?

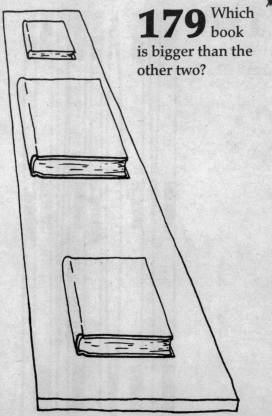

180

Can you
read it?

181

Flick the corners of the book to see the animals change. How many different animals can you count?

What are the cats trying to tell you?

VISUAL TRICKS
ANSWERS

The following pages have explanations and pictorial answers to solve the puzzles contained within this book.

1 This is a famous trick invented by Sam Loyd. The legs, arms, and bodies on the disk match up with those on the outside; however, when the disk is turned, the parts still match but make one figure less.

2 The second lamp on the left in the top row and the second from last in the second row.

3 The message reads: "Reader, before you judge you should open your soul to my defence."

4 Neither. The spider and the butterfly are the same distance from the line.

5 It is not possible to tell when you begin to count them; some spaces turn into legs.

6 There are twelve people at the party.

7 The lady on the right is a brunette, the lady on the left a blonde -- both share the same eye.

8 They could not have built it. Every time you look at the shapes they seem connected in different ways.

9 Turn the page upside down to see a different person.

10 The corner columns of the top floor seem to be directly above those on the lower floor, but on the top floor the front of the building is on the left of the picture and on the bottom floor the front of the building seems to be on the right.

11 Turn the page upside down and you will find seven animals. Their locations are revealed in picture answer 11.

12 It's amazing but those in A are real squares, those in B are distorted so that they look square.

13 The middle bill is a fake. The words say "Twenty Dollars" but the numbers say 25. Look at picture answer 13.

14 The regular distortion in the lines makes the surface look as if it's rolling up and down.

15 Hold the page so that the left-hand edge is at the bottom. Then turn it so that the right-hand edge is at the bottom.

16 As the black and white shapes get smaller and smaller, they seem to get less distinct and form gray areas.

17 Turn the page upside down.

18 Turn the page so that the left-hand edge is at the bottom and you will see the lovers' faces in the sky and water.

19 Turn the page upside down and then hold the edge close to your eye. The shape does not form words; it is the alphabet.

20 Six letters: WMHEGO. I bet you forgot about the encircling O.

21 The bomber on the right-hand side is bigger.

22 Both the buckets are the same size.

23 This is a wonderful visual trick drawn by Gustave Verbeek. If you turn the page upside down you will find his granddaughter.

24 Each state seal has a different error on the facing page. Look at picture answer 24.

25 The sign repeats the letter A: one on the second line and one on the third.

26 Simply turn the page upside down.

27 Slowly bring the pages closer and closer to your face and the center arch disappears.

28 It reads: "Choose a job that you like and you will not have to work a day in your life."

29 Another two-faced visual trick.

30 The regular pattern of black squares with narrow white spaces between them form, in your mind's eye, gray patches at the corners of the black squares.

31 Turn the page upside down and if Frank is not clear, see picture answer 31 to find out where he is.

32 Both spoons are the same size.

33 Turn the page so that the right-hand edge is at the bottom. If you still cannot find his cat, look at picture answer 33.

34 There are ten cats, look at picture answer 34 if you cannot find them.

35 The monkey labelled C. All the monkeys hold their left hands up to their mouths, monkey C holds his right hand up.

36 Hold the book up to your eye level and look across the page from the right-hand edge. It reads "PRESIDENT OF THE UNITED STATES."

37 You cannot have five candles filling a seven-candle holder. The illusion is caused by confusing the candles with the spaces between them.

38 Simply turn the page upside down to see the second facial expression.

39 The lines on the disks are vertical – it's the background that slopes.

40 Although it does not look it, the arches are the same on both sides. Look at picture answer 40 for the drawing without the column in the center.

41 There are 36 blocks in the top shape and 48 in the bottom one.

42 Hold the left-hand edge to your eye level and you will see Britain and the United States.

43 Bob. Lauren's poles are further apart at the top.

44 The fly can be on either side of the log, depending on how you look at it. If you focus on the edge at the bottom of the picture, the fly is on the top side of the log. If you focus on the top side of the log, then the fly appears to be on the bottom of the log.

45 If you turn the page so that the left edge is at the bottom, hold it at arms length, and squint, you can see Mount Rushmore.

46 He is lying on the ground – check out picture answer 46.

47 Turn the page so that the right-hand side is at the bottom. Then you may recognize the shapes. If you don't, see picture answer 47.

48 It's not a spiral, it's a set of rings within rings.

49 Turn the page upside down to find him.

50 The center die has two sides marked five (5).

51 Can you find the sixteen changes before you look at picture answer 51?

52 Both patterns are exactly the same. Peter's look as though they are built up and Martha's pressed into the sand because the shadows are positioned differently.

53 The middle bill. The twenty - dollar bill has Jackson's face, not Grant's. Look at visual trick No. 13 or look at a twenty - dollar bill.

54 They are circles but they appear irregular.

55 Where the lines cross they form patterns which do not exist but seem to form waves.

56 Turn the page upside down and look across the surface. There are ten dogs.

57 The letters are on the other side of the door; they say "WAY OUT."

58 The lines are bent inward. If they were straight the background would make them look bent. See visual trick No. 89.

59 Did you find all twelve? Check picture answer 59.

60 Both, depending on whether you are reading across or down.

61 Turn the page upside down to find the owner.

62 Yes. The background makes them look different but they are the same.

63 How many did you find? Check your discoveries with picture answer 63.

64 The gaps between the trees form the figures. Look at picture answer 64.

65 All the ropes are the same length.

66 The clowns at the top have the longer ropes.

67 You cannot fix the pieces together. Look at the ends of the piece on the top and the piece on the bottom. The piece on top is not directly above the piece on the bottom -- it just seems to be when you look at the middle of the image.

68 As the black and white shapes get smaller toward the middle, they seem to bend the surface of the page.

69 Turn the page to the right and look across it from the edge. The shapes will read "NEW YORK CITY."

70 Turn the page upside down to see.

71 See picture answer 71 to find him.

72 David can see four glasses or three bottles.

73 Hold the lower edge close to your eyes, look across the page, and you will see six cats.

74 The message reads: "I ate too many candies which leaves none for you."

75 Yes, the stripes make the dot seem closer to the bottom, but it is in the center.

76 Both pens are the same size.

77 Did you spot all seven? See picture answer 77 to find out what they are.

78 The Marx Brothers. Turn the page so that the left-hand side is close to your eyes and look across the page.

79 All the inner circles are the same shade of gray, only the outside circles change.

80 The one at the top.

81 It's Charlie Chaplin. Turn the page

upside down and look across it from the edge.

82 The middle one. It should read "THE UNITED STATES _OF_ AMERICA". See picture answer 82.

83 Both scribbles are the same length.

84 The top picture says "AROUND TO IT." The bottom picture says "EMANATE."

85 Neither. The left-hand S and 8 have a narrow top and the right-hand ones a narrow bottom.

86 Were you able to find all nineteen? Check your discoveries with picture answer 86.

87 Nobody can, it's a visual trick.

88 All the lines are the same length.

89 The lines are straight.

90 Turn the page upside down to find out.

91 Their arrangement is impossible, the drawing is a visual trick.

92 Turn the page upside down.

93 Did you find eight differences? Check your discoveries with picture answer 93.

94 The closer the tiny patterns are the more they merge.

95 The blocks are not in any possible real arrangement.

96 The stripes in the top picture are all the same width. Some of the stripes in the bottom picture are wider at one edge than the other.

97 Turn the page so that the left-hand edge is at the bottom and you will find the missing sailor, or consult picture answer 97.

98 Did you spot all twenty? Check your discoveries with picture answer 98.

99 The numbers sometimes refer to balconies and sometimes to the gaps between the balconies.

100 He is near the fire. You can find him in picture answer 100.

101 Turn the book so that you look across the page from the right-hand edge, and it will read "ILLINOIS."

102 Both. Look from the left side for Susan's and the right for Pamela's.

103 There are six. See picture answer 103.

104 Both A1 and A2 finish at B.

105 How many of the twelve did you find? Check your discoveries against picture answer 105.

106 The pattern forms stars.

107 Both men are the same size.

108 The people spell: "CAN U READ US."

109 From Sam's side 32; from Joseph's side 31.

110 What Tom and Lenny are building is impossible.

111 The circles are always circles. It's the background that makes them look like ovals.

112 No she doesn't. She is always the same size.

113 No. Both columns are the same size.

114 There are twenty-six animals hiding. Check picture answer 114.

115 When the doors close they read "NO SMOKING."

116 When the arms of the scissors are open the blades are shut.

117 Both pyramids are the same size.

118 All the plowed rows are parallel; they only look broader or narrower because of the marks in their sides.

119 The message reads: "MIMICRY IS THE SINCEREST FORM OF FLATTERY."

120 There are five faces. If you cannot find them look at picture answer 120.

121 Iris has two right hands and Josh has six fingers on his right hand.

122 Did you find twenty differences? Check picture answer 122.

123 The mark on Peter's wheel does not go round and round. It hops forward as the wheel goes along the ground. Check it out in picture answer 123.

124 No –- it's another visual trick.

125 Turn the page so that the right-hand side is at the bottom and you will see the frog.

126 The cars will not meet because they are on different ramps.

127 It reads: "UNITED STATES OF AMERICA." Turn the page so that the right-hand edge is at eye level and look across the page.

128 The top bill reads "_10_ DOLLARS" and the others read "_TEN_ DOLLARS." Check it out in picture answer 128.

129 Maybe you see the old lady and have difficulty seeing the young girl.

130 Both are the same size.

131 The cat and dog are hard to find. If you cant do it, check them out in picture answer 131.

132 Turn her upside down.

133 If Scott turns to his left, he walks down to Mike. If he turns to his right, he walks up to Mike.

134 The strange shapes read: "CAN U READ THIS PAGE EASILY?"

135 The end near the head has five upright bars. The end near the foot only has four, but the gaps and the bars are the same width at both ends.

136 He was reading an upside-down watch. Turn the page around to read the real time.

137 If you count the heads there are five children, but if you count the bodies there are ten. Check it out in picture answer 137.

138 The children are the same size as their shadows.

139 They are circles but the background makes them appear to be flattened.

140 The pattern sends out spiraling waves.

141 Hold the top edge close to your eyes and look across the page. It is George's name – WASHINGTON.

142 The black parts are the same length as the white parts of the sticks.

143 Turn the page around to see them all. Check your discoveries with picture answer 143.

144 Eight if you count the match heads on the left and only seven if you count those on the right.

145 The stack marked B.

146 No, it is much narrower at the top.

147 Turn the page upside down.

148 When turned upside down it still reads the same.

149 The hat fits in either way because it is just as high as it is wide.

150 If you look from the edge of the right-hand page you can see a map of the U.S.

151 If you look from the bottom of the page at an acute angle you should be able to read the words "ADAM AND EVE."

152 None of the shapes are circles.

153 The ant is able to get out of the maze without climbing a wall. To find out how, look at picture answer 153.

154 The middle circuit has the fault. See picture answer 154.

155 If you look from the bottom of the page at an acute angle you should be able to read the words "EYE TO EYE."

156 The seven of diamonds has eight diamonds in the center and the nine of clubs has its bottom number upside down, so they are both fake.

157 The picture is of Vincent Van Gogh.

158 The third rectangle from the left is the only one with the dot in the center.

159 It reads: "OUT FOR THE DAY." See picture answer 159.

160 There is no spiral. They are concentric circles that guide your eye to the center.

161 If you look from the edge of the right-hand page you should see the word "EYEBALL."

162 Position the page so that the bottom is farther away and you should see the word "MILWAUKEE."

163 There are two men's heads on either side of her head. Look at picture answer 163.

164 The box on the left has straight, vertical lines.

165 If you turn the page upside down you should see a head on the butterfly's wing. If you can't, look at picture answer 165.

166 No, they are not circles.

167 The outstreched fingers touch.

168 The solution is clear in picture answer 168.

169 The message reads: "It can be easy to forgive any enemy, but not to forgive a dear friend."

170 Turn the book upside down and look from the bottom right corner of the page to see Britain.

171 You can see them spiraling either way –– it depends whether you see them going away from you or coming toward you.

172 The first message reads: "I SAW A MONKEY FRIGHTEN OUR SON"; and the second message reads: "EFFICIENCY ENABLES YOU TO BE QUICK."

173 Turn the page upside down to see a horse.

174 You should see a spherical bulge forming in the center.

175 Turn the page upside down to see a different person.

176 You should see many different-sized circles overlapping and intertwining.

177 It's impossible to construct such a shape.

178 It has only one side.

179 None. The bottom two books are the same size.

180 Look across the page from the bottom edge. It reads: "EYE OPENER."

181 There are fourteen different animals. The cats' tails spell

"THE END."

11

13

24

31

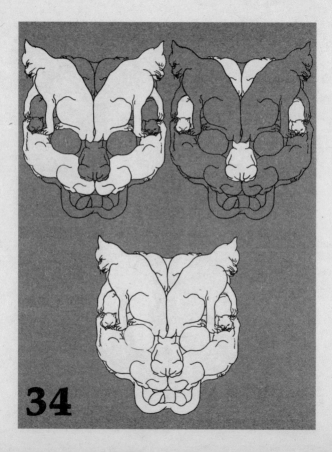

34

40

46

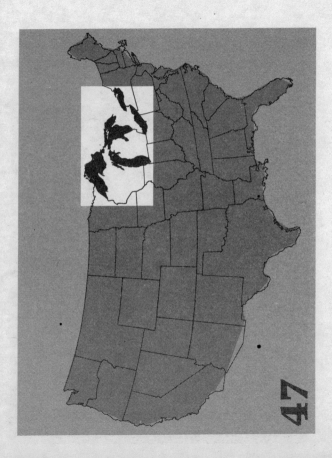

47

53

59

Wer recht bescheyden wol werden
Der pit got auff erden trumbye

63

64

71

82

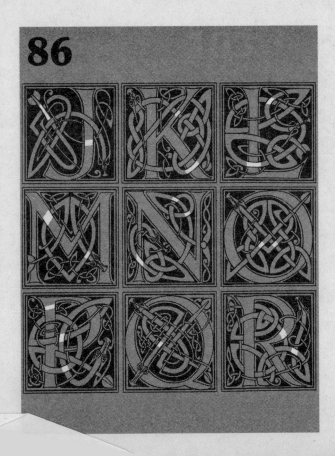

93

105

120

122

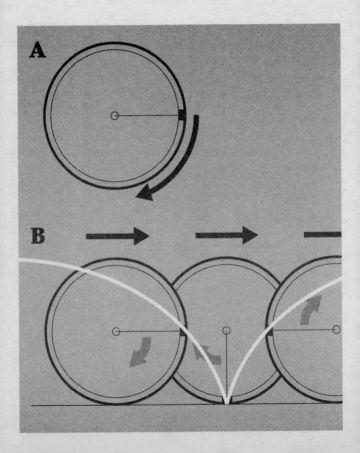

123
A If the wheel is off the ground the mark travels in a circle.
B When Peter is cycling the mark hops forward.

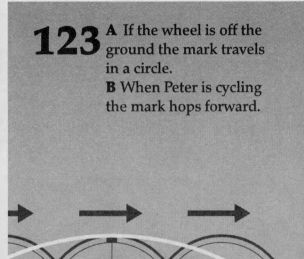

128

131

137

143

153

Cover half the maze with a sheet of paper, then count the number of lines from the middle to the outside of the maze. If you get an even number, the ant can crawl out, if odd, he must cross a line. This solution works for all closed mazes of this type.

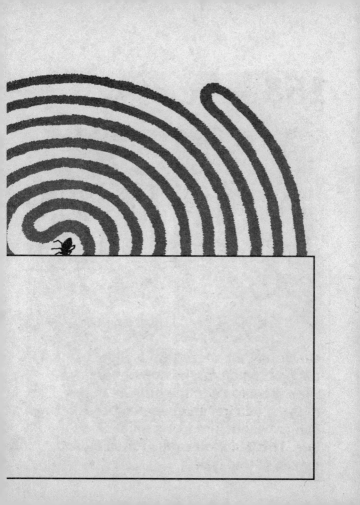

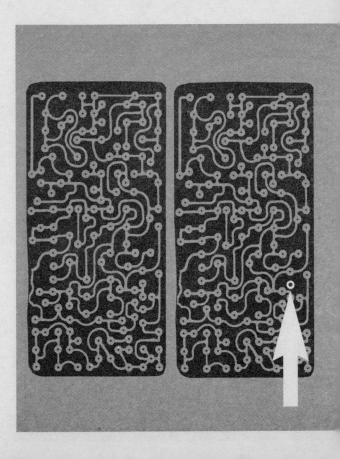

154

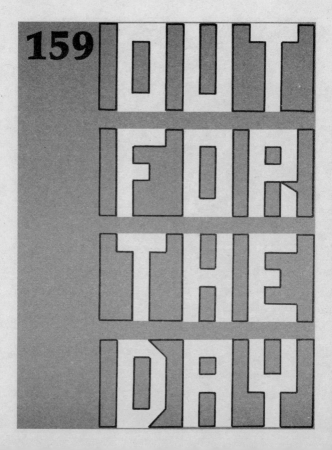

159

OUT
FOR
THE
DAY

163

165

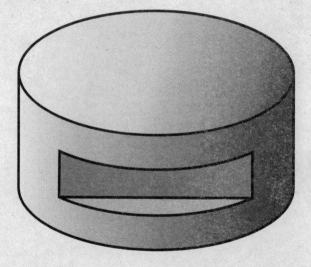